MW01295894

John F. Kennedy

A Captivating Guide to the Life of JFK

Contents

Free Bonus from Captivating History (Available for a Limited time)

Hi History Lovers!

Now you have a chance to join our exclusive history list so you can get your first history ebook for free as well as discounts and a potential to get more history books for free! Simply visit the link below to join.

Captivatinghistory.com/ebook

Also, make sure to follow us on:

Twitter: @Captivhistory

Facebook: Captivating History: @captivatinghistory

Introduction

Gallup's List of Widely Admired People of the Twentieth Century places President John F. Kennedy in the third slot, behind Martin Luther King, Jr., and Mother Teresa. Needless to say, President Kennedy's name is one that will not soon be forgotten.[i] Many people will simply recall him as the handsome president who reigned for a short while before his unfortunate death at the hands of an assassin in Dallas, Texas. They may recall he was the youngest president to have been sworn into the presidential office or he dealt with issues such as the Cuban Missile Crisis. The general American public and the world know much about the surface of JFK's life—they know of his affairs and his ill health—but they often do not recall anything about who he was as a person or how he interacted with his wife and family.

John F. Kennedy was groomed from a young age for great things. When his older brother died, Kennedy's father began prepping JFK for life in politics. John F. Kennedy did not just happen to stumble upon fame and high positions in the American government. Rather, he struggled throughout his adult life through numerous health problems and personal issues to become the leader that people remember, and his father helped him throughout the whole process both emotionally and financially.

On 20 January 1961, John F. Kennedy was sworn into office as the thirty-fifth President of the United States of America. With that position came a heavy task: he was to lead a nation filled with people who lived on the brink of the media's explosion. President Kennedy was about to enter a world in which every detail of his life was on display. Regardless, John F. Kennedy entered his presidency with vigor. In his inaugural address, JFK said all Americans needed to serve as active citizens for their country: "Ask not what your country can do for you; ask what you can do for your country." He asked that nations across the world join together so that they may fight what he referred to as the "common enemies of man: tyranny, poverty, disease, and war itself." President Kennedy said, "All this will not be finished in the first one hundred days. Nor will it be finished in the first one thousand days, nor in the life of this Administration, nor even perhaps in our lifetime on this planet. But let us begin." Closing his speech, John F. Kennedy called for greater unity among nations of the world: "Finally, whether you are citizens of America or citizens of the world, ask of us here the same high standards of strength and sacrifice we ask of you."

Through this speech, John F. Kennedy set a new precedent for the American government. He called for change, enthusiasm, nationalism, and structure. His administration was to chart a new course in foreign affairs and domestic policy. Additionally, he spotlighted himself with this speech. While the media would have still paid great attention to his comings and goings, they now paid special mind to his daily political realities both abroad and in the United States. In contrast to Eisenhower, President Kennedy's organization was structured like that of a wheel: each spoke led directly to him as he sat in the center and controlled everything. President John F. Kennedy made quick decisions and kept a variety of experienced and inexperienced people within his Cabinet, allowing the combined knowledge to lead him in various ways and in paths that previous presidents would not have considered. "We can learn our jobs together," he said.[ii]

President John F. Kennedy preferred to live in the moment. He focused on the immediate issues affecting the country and the White House, and he found he often admonished impatient people who wanted him to ponder the deeper issues pervading the administration. When Walt Whitman Rostow, the Deputy National Security Advisor, spoke of the problem with communism's continuous growth, the young President Kennedy cut him off and asked, "What do you want me to do about that today?"[iii] Overall, President Kennedy was a short-lived but effective president. While in the presidency, he made a lot of changes in the United States. He set his goals, and he geared toward them as strongly as he could. This book will provide an outline of John F. Kennedy's life while also offering a glimpse into his thoughts on politics, the way he interacted with those he loved, and the lasting impact he made on the United States of America.

Chapter One: Childhood and Education

John Fitzgerald Kennedy entered the world on 29 May 1917 at 83 Beals Street in Brookline, Massachusetts. His father was Joseph Patrick "Joe" Kennedy, a businessman and politician. John Kennedy's mother was Rose Elizabeth Fitzgerald Kennedy. Both parents came from good, well-established backgrounds. Each of John F. Kennedy's grandfathers—P.J. Kennedy and Boston Mayor John F. Fitzgerald—were politicians in Massachusetts. Additionally, all four of his grandparents were children of Irish immigrants, so his parents had a lot in common when they married, as they had comparable backgrounds.[iv]

Young John F. Kennedy had an older brother named Joseph, Jr., and seven younger siblings: Rosemary, Kathleen, Eunice, Patricia, Robert, Jean, and Ted. For the first ten years of his life, John F. Kennedy lived in Brookline. He attended the Edward Devotion School, the Noble and Greenough Lower School, and the Dexter School through the end of his fourth-grade education. For a while, Kennedy's father was relatively absent from his children's lives. Joe Kennedy was a businessman, and his ventures kept him away from his family for long periods of time in which he resided mostly in Hollywood and on Wall Street. In September 1927, the family moved from Boston, Massachusetts, to Riverdale, Bronx, New York.[v] The family settled there, slowly integrating into New York society. From the fifth to seventh grade, John Kennedy attended the lower campus of Riverdale Country School, a private school for boys. Then, the family moved to a more suburban area in Bronxville, New York, where they found better opportunities. Here, Kennedy was a member of Boy Scouts Troop Two and attended St. Joseph's Church.[vi] Though they spent most of their time in New York, the Kennedy family maintained their home in Hyannis Port, Massachusetts, where they spent their summers and early autumn. Additionally, they had a winter home in Palm Beach, Florida, where they spent their Christmas and Easter holidays.

For eighth grade, John began attending the Canterbury School in New Milford, Connecticut, in September 1930. Unfortunately, sickness struck him, and he had to withdraw from the school in April 1931 to have an appendectomy.[vii] In the following September, he enrolled at Choate, a boarding school in Wallingford, Connecticut, for his ninth through twelfth-grade years. Living the life of a younger brother, Kennedy was overshadowed by his older brother, Joe, Jr., who had already attended Choate for two years and was both a leading student and a football player at the school. As many younger siblings do, this shadow caused him to act out with rebellious behavior to garner attention, which attracted other notoriously mischievous students. In their most memorable act, they exploded a toilet seat with a firecracker, prompting George St. John, the headmaster of the school, to assemble students in the chapel for a meeting. Once they were all seated before him, he held up the toilet seat and admonished the "muckers" who dared to "spit in our sea." From there on out, John F. Kennedy referred to his group of comrades as "The Muckers Club," which included his friend and roommate Kirk LeMoyne "Lem" Billings.[viii]

While at Choate, John fell ill once again. He was hospitalized at New Haven Hospital in 1934, and he was so sick that doctors thought that he might have had leukemia. In June 1934, he was admitted to the Mayo Clinic in Rochester, Minnesota, where he was diagnosed with colitis.[ix] In June of the following year, Kennedy graduated from Choate as 64th in his class of 112 students, which was not very impressive to anyone, but he did manage to gather a few other accolades. When he graduated, he was the business manager of the yearbook and voted "most likely to succeed."[x]

After his high school graduation, Kennedy departed on his first abroad trip in which he traveled to London with his sister, Kathleen, and his parents. His goal was to make a few connections at the London School of Economics (LSE) where he wanted to study under Harold Laski, following in his older brother's footsteps. He spent a little while in this space before succumbing to an illness that forced his return to the United States in October of the same year.

Attempting to engage with education again, Kennedy enrolled at Princeton University, where he stayed for six weeks until he was hospitalized at Peter Bent Brigham Hospital in Boston, Massachusetts, for a gastrointestinal illness. The sick young John F. Kennedy spent time convalesced in Palm Beach, Florida, at the Kennedy family's winter home. Later on, he spent the spring of 1936 on the Jay Six cattle ranch near Benson, Arizona.[xi] Here, he worked on the 40,000-acre ranch as a ranch hand, gaining some experience alongside his brother.

In September of 1936, he enrolled at Harvard, seeking education once again. His application essay read,

"The reasons that I have for wishing to go to Harvard are several. I feel that Harvard can give me a better background and a better liberal education than any other university. I have always wanted to go there, as I have felt that it is not just another college, but is a university with something definite to offer. Then too, I would like to go to the same college as my father. To be a 'Harvard man' is an enviable distinction, and one that I sincerely hope I shall attain."[xii]

Kennedy produced Harvard's "Freshman Smoker," an on-campus paper, in that year, which a reviewer called "an elaborate entertainment, which included in its cast outstanding personalities of the radio, screen, and sports world." John F. Kennedy also tried out for the football, golf, and swimming teams, earning a spot on the varsity swimming team. In addition to swimming,

Kennedy sailed for the Star class, winning the 1936 Nantucket Sound Star Championship.[xiii] He sailed to France in July of 1937 and took his convertible with him with the goal of driving around Europe.[xiv]

Later, he sailed overseas with his father and older brother in June of 1938 to work at the American Embassy in London. At this time, his father was President Franklin D. Roosevelt's United States Ambassador to the Court of St. James.[xv] In preparation for his Harvard senior honors thesis, John F. Kennedy traveled to Europe, the Balkans, the Middle East, the Soviet Union, Germany, and Czechoslovakia. He returned to London from his trip on 1 September 1939, the day that marked the beginning of World War II, when Germany invaded Poland. Kennedy's father sent him as a representative to assist in any way he could with the survivors of the SS Athenia. Then, John F. Kennedy flew back to the United States from Foynes, Ireland, and arrived in Port Washington, New York. All in all, he experienced a busy couple of years while attending college.

While he was an upperclassman at Harvard College, John F. Kennedy fed his growing interest in politics and philosophy, starting to learn all the information he would need later in life. His thesis, "Appeasement in Munich," which he completed in 1940, was about how Britain chose to participate in the Munich Agreement. The book outlined how Britain neglected its military's strength in the time leading up to World War II and put out a call for an Anglo-American alliance against the rising totalitarian powers. Under the title *Why England Slept*, the published thesis grew popular and hit the bestseller list.[xvi] While writing this book, Kennedy was further developing his ideologies within the political realm, starting to formulate opinions that he would carry throughout his life. The future President John F. Kennedy heavily supported the United States' intervention in World War II, which his father Joseph did not appreciate. Due to his father's isolationist beliefs, Joseph Kennedy was relieved of his duties as ambassador to the United Kingdom. This dismissal created a barrier between the Roosevelt and Kennedy families.[xvii]

John F. Kennedy graduated cum laude in 1940 with a Bachelor of Arts degree in government from Harvard College. Unsurprisingly, his degree concentrated heavily on international affairs. In the fall, he enrolled at the prestigious Stanford Graduate School of Business where he audited classes.[xviii] He did not spend too long at Stanford, though. He left the school in early 1941, and his father enlisted his help in writing a memoir of his three years as an American ambassador. After he finished this project, Kennedy traveled around South America for a while, visiting Ecuador, Peru, and Colombia.[xixxx]

Chapter Two: Personal Life

President John F. Kennedy's adult family life is wide open to discussion. The media surrounded them at almost all times, fascinated with JFK's handsome features and politics, while also mesmerized by Jacqueline Kennedy's style choices when they were in the White House. Needless to say, John F. Kennedy's personal life is well-known today, deriving from personal accounts, media sources, and the family's own writings. As one of the most established political families in the history of the United States, they had plenty of media coverage outside of their time in the White House, as well. The family produced a president, three senators, an ambassador, and a line of other representatives within the federal government and state governments. The Kennedy line stretches far and wide.

John F. Kennedy was introduced to Jacqueline Lee "Jackie" Bouvier (1929—1994) when he was a congressman by journalist Charles L. Bartlett at a dinner party. They married on 12 September 1953, a year after he was elected senator. In 1957, they had Caroline Bouvier Kennedy, their first child. Teasingly nicknamed "John-John" by the press, John Fitzgerald Kennedy, Jr., was born 17 days after JFK was elected president in 1960.

JFK and his wife were very popular within media culture for a myriad reasons. They were younger than any of the previous presidential families and therefore garnered much attention with their youth, youthful styles, and activities. Their faces appeared on various magazines and newspapers every day. Never at one point could any member of their family go out without finding themselves bombarded with cameras or reporters. Additionally, Kennedy was the first president to fully utilize the benefits of television. Although Eisenhower televised press conferences, John F. Kennedy was the first to have his press conferences broadcast to a live audience, which allowed for no editing of the film. In this way, the audience felt more closely connected to the president. In fact, in honor of President Kennedy's open relationship with the media, the Radio-Television News Directors Association presented him with the Paul White Award. Additionally, Jacqueline Kennedy gained notoriety and media attention for her restoration of the White House as she was continuously directing the placement of new art and furniture within the historic building. The media absolutely loved the Kennedy family.

The new family was so popular with the media their names and activities popped up numerous times in popular culture, as well. For example, The Twistin' Kings called their song "Twisting at Christmas" also by the name "Twisting at the White House," and people loved it. Additionally, Vaughn Meader's *First Family* comedy album parodied the presidential family and the administration. A popular album, it sold about four million copies. The

Kennedy family also caught the attention of Marilyn Monroe, the popular actress and singer, and the woman with whom John F. Kennedy is rumored to have had an affair. At a party in Madison Square Garden on 19 May 1962, she sang "Happy Birthday, Mr. President" in celebration of JFK's upcoming 45th birthday.

While he was trying to live his life as fully as he could, John F. Kennedy was suffering from numerous health problems. Historian Robert Dallek in 2002 wrote an extensive and very detailed history of President Kennedy's health. He carefully studied a collection of papers that outlined the Kennedy family from 1955—1963. These papers included medical records such as x-rays and prescriptions, all of which were tucked away in the files of Dr. Janet Travell, the White House physician. These records indicate that John F. Kennedy suffered from a number of ailments during his time in the White House. He had high fevers, stomach troubles, colon and prostate issues, abscesses, adrenal problems, and high cholesterol. In Dr. Travell's notes was a "Medicine Administration Record" that catalogued President Kennedy's medications in detail: "injected and ingested corticosteroids for his adrenal insufficiency; procaine shots and ultrasound treatments and hot packs for his back; Lomotil, Metamucil, paregoric, phenobarbital, testosterone, and trasentine to control his diarrhea, abdominal discomfort, and weight loss; penicillin and other antibiotics for his urinary-tract infections and an abscess; and Tuinal to help him sleep."[xxi] Needless to say, President Kennedy had a rough time while living in the nation's most famous residence as he was continuously ill.

Quite a while after John F. Kennedy's death, it was revealed he had been diagnosed with Addison's disease, a rare endocrine disorder, at age thirty while he was serving his first term in Congress. The diagnosis was made by Sir Daniel Davis at the London Clinic.[xxii] As he was elected the youngest man to ever serve as President of the United States at 43 years old, Kennedy looked as if he should have been a picture of health. Instead, he had a more complicated medical history that anyone else who had served in the same position, but it was easy to keep the secret of his ill health under wraps.

Since the media was unable to attain the same information as they can today, Kennedy was able to conceal the worst of his medical problems from the American people. The public did not know about his issues until 1976 when authors Joan and Clay Blair disclosed the information in their book *The Search for JFK*. Kennedy had come into the White House, a sick man. His family was aware of the illnesses that had plagued him as a child, and in 1947 President Kennedy collapsed while visiting England. Davis told Pamela Churchill, Kennedy's friend, "That young American friend of yours, he hasn't got a year to live."[xxiii] Upon return to the United States, President Kennedy spread the rumor that he had had a severe recurrence of malaria he contracted in the Pacific during World War II. He was safe from the judging glare of his constituents for a short while.

It is believed that during Kennedy's 1960 presidential campaign, his endocrinologist prescribed treatments with testosterone, likely as a form of long-term steroid replacement therapy and possibly because of autoimmune disease. Additionally, Kennedy experienced very severe back pain, as evidenced by a write-up about his surgery in the American Medical Association's *Archives of Surgery*. Despite his illnesses, Kennedy presented an image of health and vitality to the United States public, making them think he was well and good when, in fact, his physical body was falling apart.

During the Vienna Summit in 1961 in which he associated heavily with Soviet Premier Nikita Khrushchev, President Kennedy appeared to have been taking a multitude of drugs—animal organ cells, steroids, vitamins, hormones, amphetamines, and enzymes—which began to influence his diplomacy. Side effects of these drugs include hypertension, nervousness, mood swings, hyperactivity, and impaired judgment.[xxiv] Scholars speculate these drugs were one of the reasons he performed so poorly in front of Premier Khrushchev.

Not only did Kennedy have to deal with the stresses of his political life, but he also had to cope with his doctors' disagreements. At one time, he was seeing three or more doctors, one of whom was Max Jacobson. Known as "Dr. Feelgood" and "Miracle Max," Jacobson was a controversial figure within the medical community. He had a reputation for administering amphetamines and other strong medications to high-profile clients for quick fixes that did not usually provide long-term solutions.[xxv] Often, Kennedy's doctors disagreed as to which types of medicine would prove most beneficial for his conditions. All wanted varying amounts of exercise and health dosages. As Kennedy was a busy man and preferred immediate gratification and relief, he often followed Max Jacobson's recommendations.

In the late months of 1961, President Kennedy's physician, George Burkley, set up gym equipment in the basement of the White House, and Kennedy started a regimented schedule of exercise in which he worked his back muscles three times per week as an attempt to gain muscle strength.[xxvi] Burkley thought the other doctors' diagnoses and treatments were little more than rubbish— medically inappropriate, in other words—and removed the President of the United States from their care, thereby stopping Jacobson's use of steroids and amphetamines. After his release from these medications, Kennedy is thought to have performed more effectively in his role as leader of the United States. Dr. Ghaemi, who later studied President Kennedy's medical records, said that when Kennedy stopped taking the drugs, there was a "correlation; it is not causation, but it may not be a coincidence either" that Kennedy's leadership abilities improved.

In addition to the health problems he was experiencing and all the doctors' problems that came along with the health issues, Kennedy watched many of his family members die, which placed additional stress on him and exacerbated his poor health. In 1944, Kennedy's older brother, Joe, Jr., died at the age of 29. He was killed during an attack in Operation Aphrodite over the English Channel during World War II. The president's younger sister Rose Marie "Rosemary" Kennedy, born in 1918, suffered from intellectual disabilities and underwent a prefrontal lobotomy when she was only 23 years old. The surgery left her permanently incapacitated. Another of his younger sisters, Kathleen "Kick" Kennedy Cavendish, died in a 1948 plane crash in France. Kennedy and Jacqueline also had two deceased children and a miscarriage. Jacqueline suffered a miscarriage in 1955, which was quickly followed by a stillbirth, a daughter they named Arabella, in 1956. Then, their son, Patrick Bouvier Kennedy, died only two days after birth in August 1963.

Chapter Three: Relationship with Jackie Kennedy

Of course, it is no secret that John F. Kennedy and Jacqueline Kennedy had marital issues, as evidenced by the fact that both husband and wife were rumored to have engaged in extramarital affairs. With the president, the list of affairs begins before he was married to Jacqueline. In the 1940s, Kennedy was still a single man. During this time, he is reported to have engaged in affairs with two high-profile women, Danish journalist Inga Arvad and actress Gene Tierney.[xxvii][xxviii] These affairs gained some media speculation but were nothing in comparison to the accusations he received after his marriage to Jacqueline.

Later in his life, Kennedy was reported to have had extramarital affairs with women who ranged from celebrities to White House employees. Some include Marilyn Monroe, Gunilla von Post, Judith Campbell, Mary Pinchot Meyer, Marlene Dietrich, Mimi Alford, and even Jacqueline's secretary, Pamela Turnure. The relationship with Monroe is a bit vague, but reports claim they spent a weekend together at Bing Crosby's house in March 1962. Additionally, the White House switchboard documents calls from her during 1962.[xxix] On the other hand, his relationship with Pamela Turnure, probably the most easily accessible affair, is relatively solid information.

Somehow, most of Kennedy's affairs remained relatively unimportant to the media as the media was much less invasive during this era. Perhaps it was because his time in the White House was so short. Perhaps it was because many other important things were happening around him. Regardless, most of his affairs were not completely unearthed in detail until after his death. According to Richard Reeves, President Kennedy inspired an intense loyalty from his supporters and the members of his team, loyalty which included their discretion with "the logistics of Kennedy liaisons…[which] required secrecy and devotion rare in the annals of the energetic service demanded by successful politicians."[xxx] In other words, they kept their knowledge to themselves when questioned by the media.

Jacqueline had an important role in Kennedy's presidency. Wherever he went, she also went. She made great impressions on many foreign dignitaries and leaders, tightening United States relations with other nations. When they visited Paris on their way to the Vienna Summit, Jacqueline charmed Charles de Gaulle. After leaving, President Kennedy said he would be remembered in France as "the man who accompanied Jackie Kennedy to Paris."[xxxi]

Chapter Four: Naval Service

Due to his chronic lower back problems, John F. Kennedy was rejected from the Army's Officer Candidate School in 1940, but he was determined to make his mark on the United States military. Over the next few months, Kennedy exercised and trained to straighten his back, working to relieve the pain and problematic weakness. His hard work paid off in the end; on 24 September 1941, Kennedy joined the United States Naval Reserve with the help of the Director of the Office of Naval Intelligence (ONI), the former naval attaché to his father, Joseph Kennedy. On 26 October 1941, Kennedy was commissioned as an ensign, and he joined the staff of the Office of Naval Intelligence in Washington, D.C.

Future President John F. Kennedy moved to the Office of Naval Intelligence field office at Headquarters, Sixth Naval District, in Charleston, South Carolina, in January 1942. Continuing on the path he chose for himself, he attended the prestigious Naval Reserve Officer Training School at Northwestern University in Chicago, Illinois, from 27 July to 27 September. Then, he voluntarily entered the Motor Torpedo Boat Squadrons Training Center in Melville, Rhode Island. Kennedy was beginning to carve out a name for himself, and on 10 October, he was promoted to lieutenant junior grade, a good upgrade for the amount of time he had put into the Navy. On 2 December, he completed his training and was assigned to Motor Torpedo Squadron FOUR.

Kennedy's first command was *PT-101* and lasted from 7 December 1942 until 23 February 1943. Interestingly enough, the PT (patrol torpedo) boat had been used for training while Kennedy was an instructor at Melville. After the end of this command, he led three Huckins PT boats—*PT-98, PT-99,* and *PT-101*—that were being relocated from MTBRON 4 in Melville, Rhode Island, back to Jacksonville Florida, alongside and in addition to the MTBRON 14. When Kennedy discovered a propeller was stuck, he dove into the cold water to fix it, but immediately fell ill. After his heroic moment, he was briefly hospitalized. When this trip reached a conclusion, Kennedy was sent to Panama and later to the Pacific theater where he commanded two more PT boats.

One of the most famous stories from this part of Kennedy's life involves his time on an island within the Solomon Islands. Kennedy was assigned to Motor Torpedo Squadron TWO in April 1943 and on 24 April took command of *PT-109,* a patrol torpedo that was based on Tulagi Island in the Solomon Islands. On the night of 1 August, while Kennedy was patrolling near New Georgia, he saw a nearby Japanese Destroyer and attempted to attack. Suddenly, *PT-109* was rammed by the destroyer Amagiri, which cut the boat in half, killing two crew members. Kennedy gathered the surviving crew members, which numbered at ten men, around the wreckage and asked them all to vote on whether they would surrender or fight. He said, "There's nothing in the book about a situation like this. A lot of you men have families, and some of you have children. What do you want to do? I have nothing to lose." They swam to a nearby island about three miles away.[xxxii] Unsurprisingly, the wreck injured Kennedy's already frail back, but he managed to swim the whole way while towing a badly burned crewman. Even more, he had to drag the crewman with a life jacket clenched in his teeth. The men later swam to a second island where they were rescued on 8 August. Kennedy and his executive officer on *PT-109*, Ensign Leonard Thom, were awarded the Purple Heart Medal for injuries and the Navy and Marine Corps Medal for heroism.

Although the medals Kennedy received were very honorable, he felt that the Navy and Marine Corps Medal was not meant for combat and asked that he should be considered for the Silver Star Medal. In 1950, the Department of the Navy offered Kennedy a Bronze Medal Star but said he would have to return his Navy and Marine Corps Medal to receive it. Kennedy declined. The Navy later offered the Bronze Star again, and Kennedy repeated his original request for consideration for the Silver Star Medal. The Navy declined. They were at a very odd standstill.

Kennedy took a while to recover from his injury, but nothing could keep him from his duties for long. Kennedy later returned to active duty, taking command of the *PT-59*—a patrol torpedo boat that was converted to a gunboat—on 1 September 1943. Kennedy was promoted to lieutenant in October, and on 2 November 1943, Kennedy's *PT-59* helped another boat to rescue eighty-seven stranded marines who were being held by the Japanese on two rescue landing crafts on the Warrior River at Choiseul Island, making Kennedy the heroic character once again.[xxxiii]

Under orders from his doctor, Kennedy was released from command of *PT-59* on 18 November, and he returned to the United States of America in early January 1944. He received treatment for his back injury, spending May to December in Chelsea Naval Hospital, and was completely released from active duty in late 1944. His condition had worsened so exponentially that he spent three more months in recovery in early 1945 at Castle Hot Springs, a resort that also functioned as a temporary military hospital in Arizona.[xxxiv]

When asked later how he became a war hero, Kennedy replied, "It was easy. They cut my PT boat in half."[xxxv] Kennedy also received the American Campaign Medal, the Asiatic-Pacific Campaign Medal with 3/16" bronze stars, and the World War II Victory Medal.

Chapter Five: Congressional Career

After his service in the United States Navy, John F. Kennedy and his father began to think about his future in the American political realm. Up until his death, Kennedy's oldest brother had been on the path for the family's political future. According to Robert Dallek, when his brother's plane crashed, Kennedy was suddenly thrust to the forefront as the oldest son and therefore the one who would have to carry on the Kennedy family's name. Therefore, the Kennedy patriarch, Kennedy's father, determined that John F. Kennedy would seek the presidency.[xxxvi]

Under the thumb and urging of Kennedy's father in 1946, the United States Representative James Michael Curley became mayor of Boston and vacated his seat in the Eleventh Congressional district in Massachusetts. John F. Kennedy easily filled the vacant seat. With the Kennedy family's finances and his father's ability to run a campaign, John F. Kennedy won the Democratic primary with 12% of the vote in competition with ten other candidates. Even though Republicans took control of the House in the 1946 elections, Kennedy beat his Republican opponent and took 76% of the vote. Alongside Richard Nixon and Joseph McCarthy, Kennedy and several other World War II veterans were elected to Congress for the first time that year.[xxxvii]

While the future President Kennedy served within the House of Representatives for six years, he was a part of the Education and Labor Committee and the Veterans' Affairs Committee. For much of his time in the House, he focused on international affairs and supported the Truman Doctrine as the best possible response to the emerging crisis of the Cold War. He supported the Immigration and Nationality Act of 1952, which required all incoming Communists to register with the government, and he despised the "Loss of China," a phrase which referred to the Communist Party's taking over of mainland China in 1949. Additionally, he supported public housing and was strictly opposed to the Labor Management Relations Act of 1947, a movement that restricted the power of labor unions.

As early as 1949, Kennedy began preparing for his campaign for the Senate election of 1952 in which he would face the Republican three-term incumbent Henry Cabot Lodge, Jr. Again, Joseph Kennedy financed the candidacy, and during this campaign, Robert Kennedy, John F. Kennedy's younger brother, was an important member of Kennedy's team. Kennedy defeated Lodge by 70,000 votes for the Senate seat in an impressive win.

Over the next couple of years, John F. Kennedy's endurance was tested as he underwent several spinal surgeries, which left him incapacitated and unable to serve in his roles within the government. At times, he received Catholic last rites on the occasions when he was critically ill and near death. Due to his dramatic fluctuations in health, he was often absent from the Senate to the irritation and worry of other members and his constituents. In his free time of convalescence, Kennedy published *Profiles in Courage*, a book that provided life details for United States Senators who risked their careers in pursuit of their personal beliefs. For this book, he won the Pulitzer Prize for Biography in 1957. Some rumors said his speechwriter and adviser Ted Sorensen helped to write the book, which was confirmed in Sorensen's 2008 autobiography.

During the 1956 Democratic National Convention, the future President Kennedy delivered the nominating speech for the party's presidential nominee, Adlai Stevenson II.[xxxviii] Stevenson preferred the convention select the vice-presidential nominee, and Kennedy finished second in the balloting with Senator Estes Kefauver of Tennessee coming ahead of him. Regardless, Kennedy still gained national exposure as a result of his run for the nomination.

Kennedy had other things to worry about without the stress of the vice-presidential nomination. During his time in the Senate, President Eisenhower presented the bill for the Civil Rights Act of 1957.[xxxix] Many people thought Kennedy was attempting to appease Southern Democratic opponents of the bill when he cast a procedural vote. In the end, he voted for Title III of the act, which would have granted the Attorney General powers to enjoin, but the Majority Leader, future vice president, and president Lyndon B. Johnson, agreed to let the provision die as a compromise measure. Kennedy then voted for Title IV, which was dubbed the "Jury Trial Amendment." Quite a few Civil Rights advocates said that vote would weaken the act, rather than give it more power. Eventually, Kennedy supported a final compromise bill, which passed in September 1957.[xl]

Kennedy was re-elected to a second term in the Senate in 1958, successfully defeating his Republican opponent, Boston lawyer Vincent J. Celeste, by a huge margin of 874, 608 votes in all. At that time, this election held the largest ever margin in Massachusetts politics. During the re-election campaign, Kennedy's press secretary, Robert E. Thompson, helped Kennedy's fame soar; Thompson put together a film entitled *The U.S. Senator John F. Kennedy Story*, which showcased Kennedy's life in the White House, the inner workings of his job, and his home life with his family. At the time, the film was considered a comprehensive overview of Kennedy's story. After his re-election to the Senate, Kennedy began preparing for a 1960 presidential campaign, already looking forward to ways in which he could change America for the better.[xli]

Chapter Six: 1960 Presidential Race

On 2 January 1960, John F. Kennedy announced his intentions to run for the Democratic presidential nomination. Some people questioned his youth and inexperience, but Kennedy won over large crowds of supporters with his eloquence and charisma. JFK's biggest obstacle in winning the nomination was not his inexperience or his youth but rather his Catholicism because the religion represented a minority in America. Many Americans held anti-Catholic attitudes and looked down on his religious choices, but Kennedy's vocal and heavy support of the separation of church and state helped to calm the problem. Kennedy's religion helped him win a devoted following from many Catholic voters.

A few other obstacles were represented by Kennedy's challengers for the Democratic nomination: Adlai Stevenson, Senator Hubert Humphrey, and Senate Majority Leader Lyndon B. Johnson. Kennedy worked rather hard. He purposefully traveled all over the country to build his support among the nation's democratic supporters and voters. Party officials controlled most of the delegates, but Kennedy spent a good amount of time campaigning in states that also held primaries, seeking to win several, which would boost his chances of winning the Democratic nomination. Effectively snuffing Humphrey's chances of winning the presidency, Kennedy won the Wisconsin and West Virginia primaries, surprising and impressing many Democrats. Still, at the beginning of the 1960 Democratic National Convention, people were not sure as to who would win the nomination when it boiled down to counting the votes.[xlii]

Upon entering the convention, Kennedy was the nominee with the most delegates, but the gap in numbers was not enough to ensure a clear win in the nomination. Stevenson, who was nominated to run for the Democratic Party in both 1952 and 1956, was popular in the party, and Johnson was not far behind him. Kennedy also faced a roadblock with former president Harry S. Truman, who worried that Kennedy was too inexperienced for the job of President of the United States. Trying to avoid a second ballot, Kennedy made sure his campaign was well-organized and strong, resulting in Kennedy's name coming out on top for the presidential nomination on the first ballot without having to go to a second.[xliii] Although his supporters and his brother were opposed to the idea, Kennedy chose Lyndon B. Johnson as his vice-presidential nominee, assuring himself the Texan Senator could help him win support from the states in the South.[xliv]

When he accepted the presidential nomination, Kennedy delivered his famous "New Frontier Speech": "For the problems are not all solved, and the battles are not all won—and we stand today on the edge of a New Frontier...But the

New Frontier of which I speak is not a set of promises—it is a set of challenges. It sums up not what I intend to offer the American people but what I intend to ask of them." On lists of great speeches, Kennedy's words in this particular speech often pop up as some of the most moving and inspirational in American history.

On the Republican side of the voters' list was Republican nominee Richard Nixon, who already held experience in the White House as the incumbent vice president. During their talks with voters, the two elected nominees focused on some of the following major issues: the dragging economy, Kennedy's Roman Catholicism, the Soviet space and missile programs, and the Cuban Revolution. Addressing his Catholic background, Kennedy told the Greater Houston Ministerial Association on 12 September 1960, "I am not the Catholic candidate for president. I am the Democratic Party candidate for president who also happens to be a Catholic. I do not speak for my Church on public matters—and the Church does not speak for me." Quite a few times, Kennedy was bristled when people assumed he would run the country poorly because of his religious background. He often threw the question back at voters, asking if they thought one-fourth of American citizens were of a lower class based purely on their Catholicism. Driving the point home, he said, "No one asked me my religion [while serving in the Navy] in the South Pacific."[xlv]

Kennedy squared off against Nixon in September and October during the first televised presidential debates in the history of the United States. Unfortunately for Nixon, he did not perform well during the televised programs. He had a sore, injured leg, and his short beard was sweating. He looked uncomfortable, tense, and ill-prepared. On the other hand, Kennedy made use of the makeup services and appeared relaxed in front of the camera, leading the television audience to favor his performance. Funny enough, radio listeners assumed that Nixon won the debate or that it was a tie since they could not see his appearance. At this moment in time, television began playing a dominant role in politics, allowing Kennedy's good looks and suave personality to help him in the presidential race.

After the first debate, Kennedy's campaign gained momentum, and he took over the lead in the polls. In the popular vote, Kennedy beat Nixon by only two-tenths of one percent, but the Electoral College voted in at 303 for Kennedy and 219 for Nixon. Kennedy would have garnered even more votes if 14 electors in Mississippi and Alabama had not refused to support him on the grounds of his strong support for the Civil Rights Movement. Along with one elector for Oklahoma, electors in Mississippi and Alabama voted for Senator Harry F. Byrd of Virginia instead. Regardless, Kennedy found his space in the presidential office. He became the youngest person ever to be elected as president, even though Theodore Roosevelt was younger when he took office after William McKinley's untimely death in 1901.[xlvi]

Chapter Seven: Presidency—Foreign Policy

John F. Kennedy did not have much time to rest between his campaign and his first days in the White House. As soon as he entered the presidency, he engaged with numerous issues. Confrontations with the Soviet Union were not the least of his worries as the earliest stages of the Cold War were setting in. In 1961, Kennedy planned a summit to meet with Soviet Premier Nikita Khrushchev. Unfortunately, the president made an ill first impression when he aggressively reacted to one of Khrushchev's speeches on the Cold War. Although Khrushchev intended the speech to reach out to the Soviet Union's domestic audiences, Kennedy took it as a personal challenge, which raised tensions leading up to the Vienna Summit of June 1961.[xlvii] Charles de Gaulle, the French president, and Kennedy met in Paris on Kennedy's way to the Summit. Here, de Gaulle suggested that Kennedy ignore Krushchev's abrasiveness and instead focus on the important matters at hand. Maybe if Kennedy had taken his advice, the meeting would have gone more smoothly.

Kennedy and Khrushchev met in Vienna on 4 June 1961. The president left the meeting filled with anger and disappointment, feeling he had allowed Premier Khrushchev to bully him verbally. Khrushchev was duly impressed with Kennedy's intelligence but thought he was a weak and ineffective leader. While in the meeting, Kennedy brought up a sensitive topic: a proposed treaty between East Berlin and Moscow. He clearly stated that any treaty of the sort would be regarded as an act of war since it interfered with the United States' access rights in West Berlin. Regardless of Kennedy's threats, he soon discovered after he returned home the Soviet Union leaders were announcing their intentions to sign a treaty with East Berlin. Kennedy began preparing the country for a nuclear war; his personal belief was nuclear war had about a one-in-five chance of happening, so he wanted to make sure he was prepared for the inevitable.[xlviii]

During the weeks following the Vienna Summit, over 20,000 people who feared the Soviets' statements began to flee from East Berlin toward the western sector. Dean Acheson, Secretary of State to Harry S. Truman and unofficial advisor to John F. Kennedy, recommended a military buildup for the United States of America. Taking his advice, Kennedy announced in July 1961 his decision to increase the defense budget by 3.5 billion dollars, in addition to adding more than 200,000 additional troops. The United States claimed an attack on West Berlin would function as an attack on America, as well. John F. Kennedy's speech announcing this information received an 85% approval rating from American citizens, showing the country appreciated his firm stance.[xlix]

In the month after President Kennedy broadcasted his plans, the Soviets and East Berliners began creating a blockade, allowing no one in East Berlin to cross over into West Berlin. They built barbed wire fences around the city, which quickly escalated to become the Berlin Wall. Kennedy chose to ignore this issue as long as access between the opposing sides of Berlin was still available. Soon, though, people in West Berlin began to lose hope in the United States' defense of their wavering position. In an attempt to restore confidence, Kennedy sent Vice President Lyndon B. Johnson and a host of military personnel to convoy through West Germany in a show of strength, a journey which included passage through Soviet-armed checkpoints.[l]

On 5 May 1960, President Kennedy addressed American concerns about the Cold War at Saint Anselm College. He spoke on America's conduct in the rising War, detailing how he believed American foreign policy should be conducted toward African nations and claimed to support modern African nationalism: "For we, too, founded a new nation on revolt from colonial rule."

While Kennedy was attempting to deal with Russia, he also had another country about which to worry: Cuba. When Eisenhower was in the presidency, he and his administration created a plan to overthrow Fidel Castro's dictatorial rule in Cuba. The plan required the Central Intelligence Agency (CIA) to team with the United States military in efforts to invade Cuba with a counter-revolutionary insurgency that was made up of anti-Castro, United States-trained Cuban exiles that followed the lead of CIA paramilitary officers. Their goal was to invade Cuba, create an uprising among the Cuban people, and remove Castro from power.[li] The plan was passed along to Kennedy, who approved it on 4 April 1961. The administration began hashing out the details.

Dubbed the Bay of Pigs Invasion, the planned infiltration began on 17 April 1961. The Brigade 2506, which consisted of 1,500 United States-trained Cubans, landed on the island, with no United States air support providing backup. The director of the Central Intelligence Agency, Allen Dulles, said later the leaders on the ground assumed President Kennedy would authorize anything that would allow success for the troops once they were landed and on the ground.[lii] That did not seem to be the case, though. Within two days of their landing, the Cuban government managed to capture or kill all the invading exiles, which meant that Kennedy gained the responsibility of negotiating for the release of over 1,100 survivors, a goal for which he did not have the time or patience. Twenty months later, Cuba made an agreement with the United States government in which they released the exiles in exchange for 53 million dollars' worth of food and medicine.[liii] The incident did prove one good thing, though: Fidel Castro grew wary of the United States in fear that they would send invaders again in the future.

Biographer Richard Reeves argues that during the Bay of Pigs Invasion and its execution, Kennedy maintained a larger focus on the political repercussions of his plan, paying less attention to the military issues that came along with it.

When the plan failed, he became quite aggravated and assumed people were conspiring against him to make him look bad as a leader of the United States.[liv] Regardless, President Kennedy took responsibility for the failure. He said, "We got a big kick in the leg, and we deserved it. But maybe we'll learn something from it."[lv] With few other options, the White House created a Special Group—led by Robert Kennedy and including Edward Lansdale and Secretary Robert McNamara—with the specific goal to take down Fidel Castro's reign through the use of espionage, sabotage, and other covert affairs. In reality, those tactics were never pursued.[lvi]

On 14 October 1962, Kennedy's two largest problems in foreign affairs—Cuba and Russia—came together in a conspiracy. Central Intelligence Agency U-2 spy planes were able to successfully photograph intermediate-range ballistic missile sites that the Soviets were building in Cuba. President Kennedy saw the pictures on 16 October. Along with a team of advisors, Kennedy reached the conclusion that the missiles were offensive and dangerous, therefore posing an immediate nuclear threat to the country and the world.[lvii] Unfortunately, a problem arose, blocking any further action. The United States had a dilemma: if they attacked the missile sites, their actions might prompt a nuclear war, but if they did nothing, the country would fall under the threat of nearby nuclear weapons while also appearing weak to the rest of the world in their defense of the hemisphere. Since Kennedy had already presented himself as a weak leader to Khrushchev, he had a lot to prove after the Vienna Summit and did not want to appear weak in this aspect, as well.[lviii]

Within the National Security Council (NSC), over a third of the members preferred a surprise air assault on the Soviet missile sites, but other members thought this action would be too reminiscent of what they called "Pearl Harbor in reverse."[lix] Some of the international community members who were privy to this possible plan thought it might seem a bit like the pot calling the kettle black in light of Eisenhower's placement of PGM-19 Jupiter missiles in Italy and Turkey in 1958. Additionally, there was no way to guarantee that an assault would prove 100 percent effective.[lx] After the National Security Council voted on the issue, President Kennedy determined that the United States would impose a naval quarantine. Then, on 22 October, he sent a message to Khrushchev with the plan included before announcing the decision publicly on television.[lxi]

According to the new plan, the United States Navy, beginning on 24 October, would halt and do a thorough inspection of all Soviet ships that arrived near Cuba, attempting to keep the Cuban government from gaining any more nuclear power than they already had. The Organization of American States, which consisted of 35 independent states of the Americas, provided unanimous support for removing the Soviet missiles, so the United States was not alone in its goals. President Kennedy and Soviet Premier Khrushchev exchanged two sets of letters but produced no real results. General U. Thant, the Secretary of the United Nations, requested that both parties try to settle back for a while in a cooling-off period before making any rash decisions. Khrushchev agreed to follow Thant's advice, but Kennedy did not.[lxii]

Only one time did the United States Navy have to stop a Soviet-flagged ship to board to search; needless to say, the plan was less fruitful than the United States government expected, but it did what it needed to do. Soon after, on 28 October, Khrushchev agreed to dismantle and disband the missile sites in Cuba under the watchful eye of United Nations inspectors. Publicly, the United States promised they would refrain from ever invading Cuba and, privately, they agreed to also remove their Jupiter missiles from their locations in Italy and Turkey, so they did not encounter the same issues again in the case of another nuclear crisis.[lxiii] At the end of the crisis, Kennedy experienced a rise in his credibility and approval ratings.[lxiv]

Kennedy was also dealing with communistic issues in Latin America. President Kennedy said, "Those who make peaceful revolution impossible will make violent revolution inevitable." In light of the perceived communist threat in Latin America, he aimed toward creating the Alliance for Progress, which provided aid to those Latin American countries that sought to garner greater human rights outside of the rule of communist governments.[lxv] He and the Governor of Puerto Rico, Luis Muñoz Marín, worked closely together to develop the Alliance for Progress with the goal of the Commonwealth of Puerto Rico's gaining autonomy.

President Kennedy had inherited the Eisenhower administration's plans to assassinate Fidel Castro. In addition to this tyrant, they were also aiming to eradicate Rafael Trujillo in the Dominican Republic, which created another issue within Kennedy's politics. Kennedy made sure the CIA knew any such plans must include plausible deniability from the United States government. In the public eye, Kennedy denied the government had planned an assassination attempt of any sort.[lxvi] In June of 1961, the leader of the Dominican Republic was assassinated; following his death, the Undersecretary of State, Chester Bowles, led a cautious reaction by the nation. Robert Kennedy, thinking quickly and seeing an opportunity for the United States, called Bowles a "gutless bastard" to his face in an attempt to create a public distaste for him.[lxvii]

Kennedy asked Congress to create the Peace Corps. Robert Sargent Shriver, John F. Kennedy's brother-in-law, was the first director of the Peace Corps.[lxviii] Within this program, American citizens volunteered to assist underdeveloped nations in education, healthcare, construction, and farming. By March 1963, the organization had grown to 5,000 members, then 10,000 in 1964.[lxix] Since 1961, over 200,000 American citizens have joined the Peace Corps, which provides services in 139 countries.[lxx]

When a new president arrives at the White House, they are briefed by the previous President of the United States on current issues and threats. When President Kennedy met with Eisenhower, the former president emphasized the communist threat in Southeast Asia, saying it needed immediate attention as a priority for the White House. Eisenhower said Laos was "the cork in the bottle." Then in March 1961, Kennedy altered the policy surrounded Laos, saying the country should be neutral, rather than free, and that Vietnam, not Laos, should be the center of America's focus as the tripwire for the spread of communism in the area.[lxxi]

President Kennedy sent Vice President Lyndon B. Johnson in May 1961 to meet with the President of South Vietnam, Ngo Dinh Diem. Johnson guaranteed the United States would provide more aid in creating a fighting force to resist the communists. After this meeting, President Kennedy announced there was to be a change in policy regarding the United States' partnership with Diem; they would join to defeat the communism that was overtaking the government in South Vietnam.[lxxii] During his administration, Kennedy continued to create policies that provided political and economic support, along with military advice and support, for the South Vietnamese government.[lxxiii] In late 1961, the Viet Cong garnered more attention on the political world scene as they seized the provincial capital of Phuoc Vinh.[lxxiv] In reaction, Kennedy increased the number of United States Special Forces and military advisors, which he utilized almost exclusively in Vietnam, from 11,000 to 16,000 over the course of two years, but he did not command a full-scale deployment of troops.[lxxv] A year and a half later, after Kennedy's death, President Lyndon B. Johnson, sent the first combat troops to Vietnam, heavily escalating the involvement of the United States. After this, forces reached 184,000 in number then 536,000 in 1968.

At the beginning of 1962, President Kennedy increased involvement in Vietnam upon signing the National Security Action Memorandum, "Subversive Insurgency (War of Liberation)."[lxxvi] Within the United States, strong supporters and strong opponents voiced their opinions on the subject of engaging with Vietnam. Dean Rusk, the Secretary of State under President Kennedy, strongly supported the involvement of the United States in Vietnam. Kennedy spoke of the situation in Vietnam in April 1963: "We don't have a prayer of staying in Vietnam. Those people hate us. They are going to throw our asses out of there at any point. But I can't give up that territory to the communists and get the American people to re-elect me."[lxxvii] Despite the weighty support of the United States, the Vietnamese military was not very effective in combatting the pro-communist Viet Cong forces. President Kennedy's crisis began with this realization. Soon after, the United States clergy on the Ministers' Vietnam Committee began expressing the first formal anti-Vietnam sentiments.[lxxviii]

In September, the White House met to discuss the impending disaster in Vietnam. General Victor Krulak of the Department of Defense and Joseph Mendenhall of the State Department provided updated assessments to the meeting after they engaged personal inspections on the ground. Krulak argued the military fight against the communists was going well, while Mendenhall said the country was slowly losing the United States' influence. After hearing their testimonies, Kennedy, unaware the two men were not speaking with one another is reported as asking, "Did you two gentlemen visit the same country?"[lxxix]

In an effort to reconcile the competing reports and to manage to formulate a policy based on fact, President Kennedy appointed Defense Secretary McNamara and General Maxwell D. Taylor to a mission in Vietnam. McNamara and Taylor were to visit the country with a goal that "emphasized the importance of getting to the bottom of the differences in reporting from U.S. representatives in Vietnam."[lxxx] Vietnam's vice president, Nguyen Ngoc Tho, told Taylor and McNamara that the military was not succeeding at all. In light of this information, Kennedy insisted that troops begin withdrawing with 1,000 leaving by the end of the year and all dispersing by 1965 since he felt like he was wasting his time and resources.

In October, international reports began suggesting that a coup against the Diem government was brewing. President Kennedy instructed the United States offer secret assistance to the coup as long as the plan did not involve assassination and the United States could deny involvement.[lxxxi] As the coup grew closer, Kennedy ordered all cables should be routed through him. He wanted complete control of the responses from the United States but also wanted to avoid affiliation through a paper trail, which put him in a difficult space.[lxxxii] Finally, South Vietnamese generals overthrew the Diem government on 1 November 1963, resulting in the arrest and killing of Diem and Nhu. President Kennedy was surprised by the assassinations but was informed the deaths were necessary since the time frame would not have worked out in any other way.[lxxxiii]

Initially, news of the coup instilled a new sense of confidence both in America and South Vietnam, and both countries considered that the war might be won. Before leaving for his ill-timed trip to Dallas, President Kennedy told Michael Forrestal, who was his National Security Advisor, that "after the first of the year, [he wanted] an in-depth study of every possible option [for the war], including how to get out of there…to review this whole thing from the bottom to the top." Forrestal translated this message as the following: "It was devil's advocate stuff."[lxxxiv]

Many historians have various opinions as to whether Kennedy's living would have escalated the Vietnam issue. In the film *The Fog of War*, Secretary of Defense McNamara said that Kennedy was strongly opposed to pulling the United States out of Vietnam after the 1964 election, assuming he would have won.[lxxxv] Lyndon Johnson claimed on tape, though, that Kennedy was planning to withdraw troops. Robert Kennedy said in 1964 that if South Vietnam had been on the brink of defeat, he and his brother would have had to "face that when we came to it." In fact, at the time of Kennedy's death, there was no clear decision about the United States future policy on how to deal with Vietnam.[lxxxvi] Theodore Sorensen wrote in 2008, "I would like to believe that Kennedy would have found a way to withdraw all American instructors and advisors [from Vietnam]. But even someone who knew JFK as well as I did can't be certain because I do not believe he knew in his last weeks what he was going to do...[Vietnam] was the only foreign policy problem handed off by JFK to his successor in no better, and possibly worse, shape than it was when he inherited it."[lxxxvii]

What we do know is that Kennedy presented the commencement address at American University in Washington, D.C., on 10 June 1963. In this speech, the President outlined a plan to curb nuclear weapons. Additionally, he "laid out a hopeful, yet realistic route for world peace at a time when the U.S. and Soviet Union faced the potential for an escalating nuclear arms race." President Kennedy wished to

"discuss a topic on which too often ignorance abounds and the truth is too rarely perceived—yet it is the most important topic on earth: world peace...I speak   of peace because of the new face of war...in an age when a singular nuclear weapon contains ten times the explosive force delivered by all the allied forces in the Second World War...an age when the deadly poisons produced by a nuclear exchange would be carried by wind and air and soil and sea to the far corners of the globe and to generations yet unborn...I speak of peace, therefore, as the necessary rational end of rational men...world peace, like community peace, does not require that each man love his neighbor—it requires only that they live together in mutual tolerance...our problems are man-made—therefore they can be solved by man. And man can be as big as he wants."[lxxxviii]

In his announcement, the president made two important notes: The Soviets wanted to negotiate a nuclear test ban treaty, and the United States postponed planned atmospheric tests.[lxxxix]

In light of France's attempt to build a Franco-West German counterweight to the American and Soviet spheres of influence, Kennedy gave a public speech in West Berlin to remind the world of America's commitment to Germany and to criticizing communism. The response was ecstatic and positive.[xc] Utilizing the Berlin Wall as an example of communism's failures, Kennedy said, "Freedom has many difficulties, and democracy is not perfect. But we have never had to put a wall up to keep our people in, to prevent them from leaving us." The speech is known for the phrase *Ich bin ein Berliner*, which translates to "I am a citizen of Berlin." Over one million people showed up on the streets of Berlin to hear the speech, and Kennedy later remarked to Ted Sorensen,

"We'll never have another day like this one, as long as we live."[xci]

Additionally, Kennedy kept a caring eye on Israel during his presidency. He initiated security ties with the country, receiving credit as the founder of the United States-Israeli military alliance. He also ended the Eisenhower and Truman administrations' and enforced an arms embargo on Israel. He said in 1960, "Israel will endure and flourish. It is the child of hope and the home of the brave. It can neither be broken by adversity nor demoralized by success. It carries the shield of democracy, and it honors the sword of freedom." Kennedy described the United States' protection of Israel as a moral and national obligation. In 1962, the President offered the first informal security guarantees to Israel and was the first president to allow Israel to buy advanced United States weaponry and to provide support for Israeli policies, such as their water project on the Jordan River, against Arab neighbors.[xcii]

President Kennedy ran into a few roadblocks with Israel during his dealings with the government. He encountered tensions with the Israeli leadership over their production of nuclear materials in Dimona; the President believed the production could instigate a nuclear arms race in the Middle East. In the beginning, the Israeli government denied the existence of a nuclear plant, and David Ben-Gurion, in a speech to the Israeli Knesset on 21 December, said that the Beersheba nuclear plant's purpose was for "research in problems of arid zones and desert flora and fauna."[xciii] Upon meeting with Kennedy in New York, Ben-Gurion claimed that Dimona would provide nuclear power for desalinization and other peaceful endeavors "for the time being."[xciv]

Later, Kennedy wrote a letter to Ben-Gurion, saying he was nervous about proceedings and that American support was on the line if Israel did not provide reliable information on their nuclear program. Ben-Gurion repeated his previous peaceful promises that all would be well, but the Israeli government resisted American insistence they open their nuclear facilities to inspection by the International Atomic Energy Agency (IAEA). By 1962, though, the United States and Israeli governments agreed to an annual inspection regime. The American leading the inspection team said the goal was to find "ways to not reach the point of taking action against Israel's nuclear weapons program."[xcv]

Unfortunately, a science attaché in the Tel Aviv embassy shared that the Israeli government temporarily shut down part of the Dimona facility to mislead the visiting American scientists.[xcvi] According to journalist and political writer Seymour Hersh, the Israeli government set up false rooms for the visiting Americans to view. Abe Feinberg, and Israeli lobbyist said, "It was part of my job to tip them off that Kennedy was insisting on [an inspection]."[xcvii] Hersh argued the conducted inspections "guaranteed that the whole procedure would be little more than a whitewash, as the President and his senior advisors had to understand: the American inspection team would have to schedule its visits well in advance and with the full acquiescence of

Israel."[xcviii] Marc Trachtenberg who is a professor of international relations at UCLA, has argued that "Although well aware of what the Israelis were doing, Kennedy chose to take this as satisfactory evidence of Israeli compliance with America's non-proliferation policy."[xcix] After much back and forth, Dimona was never placed under IAEA safeguards, and attempts to force Israel to adhere to the Nuclear Non-Proliferation Treaty continued until 1968.

Following the overthrow of the Iraqi monarchy on 14 July 1958 and the declaration of a republic government under Brigadier Abd al-Karim Qasim, relations between Iraq and the United States grew strained.[c] A couple of years after the new government was installed, Qasim installed troops on the border between Iraq and Kuwait on 25 June 1961, saying that Kuwait was "an indivisible part of Iraq," which caused a brief "Kuwait Crisis." President Kennedy, with help from the United Kingdom's endeavor to bring the dispute to the United Nations Security Council, dispatched a United States Navy task force to Bahrain. The situation was finally resolved in October, but the Qasim government passed Public Law 80 in December 1961, restricting the British- and American-owned Iraq Petroleum Company (IPC)'s concessionary holding to the oil-producing areas.

Robert Komer, the Senior National Security Council adviser, worried that if the IPC ceased production, Qasim might attempt to take Kuwait or look to Russia for help. The State Department in April 1962 issued new guidelines on Iraq with the intention to increase American influence. President Kennedy attempted to take control of the situation and instructed the CIA to make preparations for a military coup against Qasim.[ci] On 8 February 1963, the anti-imperialist and anti-communist Iraqi Ba'ath Party overthrew and then executed Qasim in a violent coup. Some rumors say that the CIA organized and executed the coup, but declassified documents and former CIA agents' testimonies claim that America was not directly involved even though the CIA was, indeed, searching the Iraqi military for a replacement for Qasim. Overall, the Kennedy administration was pleased with the outcome of the coup and approved a 55 million-dollar arms deal for Iraq.[cii]

Chapter Eight: Domestic Policy

When the new President John F. Kennedy entered the Oval Office, he entered a domestic program contract, as well. He had a lot of promises to keep: the "New Frontier" was in its earliest stages. This new domestic program promised to provide federal funding for medical care for the elderly; education, economic aid for rural areas, and, finally, government intervention to halt the recession ravaging the country. Additionally, President Kennedy was ambitious in promising to end racial discrimination through his endorsement of the Voter Education Project (VEP), which actually produced little to no progress in states such as Mississippi where racism was rampant; the "VEP concluded that discrimination was so entrenched."

When President Kennedy gave his State of the Union address in 1963, he proposed a substantial tax reform, along with a reduction in income tax rates from the 20-90% range to a lower 14-65% range. He also proposed lowering corporate tax rates from 53% to 47% and that the top rate should be set at 70% if deductions were not eliminated for high-income earners. Speaking to the Economic Club of New York in 1963, President Kennedy said, "The paradoxical truth [is] that tax rates are too high and revenues too low, and the soundest way to raise revenue in the long term is to lower rates now."[ciii] Congress did not actually move toward these goals until 1964 after Kennedy's death when they lowered the top individual rate to 70% and the top corporate rate to 48%.

Coming into power, President Kennedy ended an era of tight fiscal policies, creating monetary policies that were looser than previous presidents' ideas in order to lower interest rates and encourage economic growth.[civ] Even with his efforts, Kennedy was the first president to work with a government that topped the 100 billion-dollar mark on the national budget deficit. Additionally, in 1961, he led the country's first non-war, non-recession deficit.[cv] Regardless, the economy accelerated noticeably during his presidency after being in two recessions during three years as it turned and prospered under the Kennedy administration. According to the United States Department of Commerce, the rate of growth in GDP and industry continued until around 1969 and has yet to repeat this trend over such a sustained period of time.

During Kennedy's presidency, the United States steel industry gained attention. Robert Kennedy argued the steel executives determined together that they would fix prices, saying that "We're going for broke...their expense accounts, where they've been and what they've been doing...the FBI is to interview them all...we can't lose this."[cvi] Administration worked with U.S. Steel, convincing them to rescind the increase in prices. The *Wall Street Journal* said that the administration acted "by naked power, by threats, by agents of the state security police," and Charles Reich, a Yale law professor, said in an article in *The New Republic* that the administration violated civil liberties by so quickly calling a grand jury to indict U.S. Steel for collusion.[cvii] On the other hand, a writer for the *New York Times* praised President Kennedy's reactions, saying the steel industry's price increase "imperils the economic welfare of the country by inviting a tidal wave of inflation." The Bureau of Budget told another story: a report stated that the price increase would have allowed for a net gain in GDP, along with a net budget surplus.[cviii] Additionally, the stock market dropped 10% after the administration chose to take action against the steel industry.[cix]

President Kennedy made a few other stirs in administration policy, as well, one of which included the last federal execution prior to *Furman v. Georgia*, a 1972 case that led to a moratorium on federal executions. A federal court in Iowa sentenced Victor Feguer to death, and he was executed on 15 March 1963. Believing this mandated execution was too much, President Kennedy commuted a death sentence a military court imposed on seaman Jimmie Henderson on 12 February 1962, instead suggesting that life in prison would serve just as well. Then on 22 March 1962, Kennedy signed HR5243 (PL87-423) into law, which abolished the mandatory death penalty for first-degree murder in the District of Columbia, which was the only place in the United States that inflicted this penalty.

Kennedy, claiming he would solve the issues of state-sanctioned racial discrimination in the United States, took on a large and important burden when he entered the presidential office. As institutional racism was one of the most obvious and pressing domestic issues of the 1960s, President Kennedy had his hands full. Up until this point, Jim Crow segregation was still the established and followed law in the Deep South.[cx] In 1954, the Supreme Court of the United States ruled during the case of *Brown v. Board of Education* that racial segregation in public schools was unconstitutional. Regardless, many southern states ignored the Supreme Court's decision, along with keeping public spaces such as buses, theaters, bathrooms, beaches, restaurants, and courtrooms segregated.[cxi]

Kennedy took a strong stand, verbally supporting racial integration and Civil Rights. During his 1960 campaign, he called Coretta Scott King—the wife of the Reverend Martin Luther King, Jr., who was in jail at the time for attempting to integrate a department store lunch counter. Robert Kennedy also took action, calling Georgia Governor Ernest Vandiver to obtain MLK's release from prison; his brother's candidacy provided him additional authority in his request.[cxii] Historian Carl M. Brauer argues that attempting to pass any Civil Rights legislation in 1961 would have proved futile due to Southern Democratic control of congressional legislation.[cxiii] During his first year in office, President Kennedy attempted to integrate the White House, as well, appointing many black American citizens to office, including his May appointment of Thurgood Marshall, a Civil Rights attorney, to the federal bench.[cxiv]

President Kennedy said in January 1961, during his first State of the Union Address, "The denial of constitutional rights to some of our fellow Americans on account of race—at the ballot box and elsewhere—disturbs the national conscience, and subjects us to the change of world opinion that our democracy is not equal to the high promise of our heritage." Kennedy knew that the grassroots aspect of the Civil Rights Movement would easily anger most white people in the South, making it harder to pass Civil Rights laws, including anti-poverty legislation, in Congress; therefore, he distanced himself from it.[cxv]

Robert Kennedy suggested his brother needed to be concerned with foreign issues, rather than domestic policy and said that the administrations' early priority was to "keep the president out of this civil rights mess." Participants in the Civil Rights Movement criticized President Kennedy, saying he was lukewarm on issues, especially of concern to the Freedom Riders who were organizing an integrated public transportation system in the South and were repeatedly intimidated and harmed by white men engaging in mob violence, which included law enforcement officers at federal and state levels. In reaction, Kennedy assigned federal marshals to protect the Freedom Riders, a move which the Riders did not consider enough in light of the fact that he could have done much more.[cxvi] Speaking for the president, Robert Kennedy advised that the Freedom Riders "get off the buses and leave the matter to peaceful settlement in courts."[cxvii] The Kennedys thought that sending federal troops would exacerbate the problem and would stir up "hated memories of Reconstruction" among white conservatives in the South.[cxviii]

On 6 March 1961, Kennedy signed Executive Order 10925, which stated government contractors must "take affirmative action to ensure that applicants are employed and that employees are treated during employment without regard to their race, creed, color, or national origin," therefore establishing the President's Committee on Equal Employment Opportunity. Unhappy with the president's reluctance to address directly the issue of segregation at an admirable pace, the Reverend Martin Luther King, Jr. and his fellow fighters for justice produced a document in 1962 that called on President Kennedy to follow Abraham Lincoln's example by using an Executive Order to make Civil Rights a Second Emancipation Proclamation. President Kennedy did not follow the advice and did not execute the order.

A pivotal point in the Civil Rights Movement occurred in September 1962 when James Meredith enrolled at the University of Mississippi. When he arrived on campus, he was prohibited from entering. Attorney General Robert Kennedy's response was to send 400 federal marshals, and President Kennedy sent 3,000 troops after the campus situation grew violent in nature.[cxix] After the Ole Miss Riot of 1962 ended, two people were dead, and dozens were injured, but Meredith finally enrolled for class. President Kennedy immediately regretted his choice not to send more troops earlier and reconsidered his ideas on how to deal with integration in the South. On 20 November 1962, Kennedy finally signed Executive Order 11063, which prohibited racial discrimination in federally-supported housing or "related facilities."[cxx]

In the White House, Civil Rights conversations were getting heated. President Kennedy in early 1963 told the Reverend Martin Luther King, Jr. his thoughts on Civil Rights legislation: "If we get into a long fight over this in Congress, it will bottleneck everything else, and we will still get no bill."[cxxi] Since Civil Rights clashes were rising within politics and on the streets, Robert Kennedy and Ted Sorenson advised that President Kennedy take more initiative in the legislative fight for equality.[cxxii] When Alabama Governor George Wallace decided to block two black students, Vivian Malone and James Hood, from entering and attending the University of Alabama on 11 June 1963, President Kennedy intervened with a firm hand. Wallace moved out of the way only when confronted by Deputy Attorney General Nicholas Katzenbach and the Alabama National Guard under orders from the president.

On that night, Kennedy provided his famous Civil Rights Address on national television and through the radio, which publicly launched his initiative for Civil Rights legislation that would provide equal access to public schools and other public places, along with greater protection for voting rights.[cxxiii] Kennedy's proposals helped create the Civil Rights Act of 1964, and that same day ended with the assassination of Medgar Evers, the NAACP leader, at his home in Mississippi.[cxxiv] The Southern Democrats and Republicans immediately reacted negatively to John F. Kennedy's speech, pushing down President Kennedy's efforts in Congress. When Arthur M. Schlesinger, Jr. praised Kennedy for his speech, the president replied, "Yes, and look at what happened to area development the very next day in the House…But of course, I had to give that speech, and I'm glad that I did."[cxxv] *The New York Times* published an article on 16 June comparing President Kennedy's previous reactions to how he functioned after his speech in regard to Civil Rights: before, the president "moved too slowly and with little evidence of deep moral commitment," but he "now demonstrates a genuine sense of urgency about eradicating racial discrimination from our national life."[cxxvi]

Despite Kennedy's efforts, the discrimination problem could not be solved so easily, and American citizens were displeased with the White House's progress. Over 100,000 protestors, which consisted mostly of black Americans, gathered in the nation's capital for the Civil Rights March on Washington for Jobs and Freedom on 28 August 1963. While Kennedy supported their efforts, he feared that the march would negatively affect the prospects for Civil Rights bills to pass through Congress; therefore, he declined an invitation to speak at the gathering. He was able, though, to give some of the details of the government's involvement to the Department of

Justice, which channeled hundreds of thousands of dollars to the March's sponsors, two of them being the NAACP and MLK's Southern Christian Leadership Conference (SCLC).[cxxvii]

President Kennedy worked closely with the March organizers to ensure the demonstration would be peaceful. They personally edited speeches to remove inflammatory language and agreed the March would occur on a Wednesday and would end by four o'clock in the afternoon. Thousands of troops were on standby to make sure that the Protest would not grow violent. Afterward, the March was considered a "triumph of managed protest" as no demonstration-related arrests occurred. The president felt that the March was good for Civil Rights opportunities in the future and that it was a victory for him, bolstering chances to pass a Civil Rights bill.[cxxviii]

Just when things were looking up, the country experienced another setback. Three weeks after the March, a bomb exploded at the 16th Street Baptist Church in Birmingham on 15 September. Four black American children died in the explosion, and two other children were shot to death in the aftermath of the incident.[cxxix] In light of the violence, the Civil Rights legislation had to go through a few added amendments that hurt its chances of passing through Congress, which did not go over so well with JFK. He called the congressional leaders to the White House for a meeting, and the following day saw the original bill gain enough votes to pass through the House committee. Eventually, Kennedy's successor—Lyndon B. Johnson—enacted the legislation, which enforced voting rights, employment, education, public accommodations, and the administration of justice for all citizens of the United States.[cxxx]

Along with racial discrimination, President Kennedy also worked to tackle gender discrimination. On 14 December 1961, JFK signed the executive order that created the Presidential Commission on the Status of Women, a commission headed by former First lady Eleanor Roosevelt. The results revealed that, unsurprisingly, women had very different experiences than men within United States culture. The final Commission report, which was released in October 1963, documented legal and cultural barriers for women. On 10 June 1963, Kennedy signed the Equal Pay Act of 1963, which prohibited unequal payments based on gender, an amendment to the Fair Labor Standards Act.

Women and black Americans were not the only people Kennedy sought to assist during his administration. In his 1960 campaign, President Kennedy proposed a complete overhaul of America's policies on immigration and naturalization laws. He planned to ban discrimination on the basis of national origin, another hefty issue to take head-on. For President Kennedy, these ideas were simply an extension of his promise to ensure Civil Rights for Americans. His reforms to immigration policies became law with the Immigration and Nationality Act of 1965, which allowed the source of immigration in America to shift from European countries to Latin American and Asian nations. Policies also shifted to maintain a focus on unifying families, rather than specifically selecting individuals for immigration. JFK's brother, Senator Edward Kennedy, helped push the new legislation through the Senate.

Early in 1960, the country saw the conception of the Apollo Program under the Eisenhower administration as a follow-up to Project Mercury. The Apollo Program involved a shuttle that astronauts could use to orbit the Earth and attempt to land on the moon or, at least, orbit around it. NASA began planning for Apollo without definite funding under Eisenhower. As a United States Senator, Kennedy was opposed to the space program and desired its complete termination, but his ideas altered once in the presidency.[cxxxi]

While determining how to run his presidential administration, Kennedy chose to retain Eisenhower's science adviser, Jerome Wiesner, as the leader of the President's Science Advisory Committee.

During President Kennedy's State of the Union address in January 1961, he suggested the international community should cooperate in space exploration. Khrushchev declined, of course, because the Soviets did not wish to share their advancements in rocketry and space capabilities.[cxxxii] All of Kennedy's advisors told him any opportunities for space travel and exploration would be unnecessarily expensive, so the president was understandably nervous about the prospects. However, thanks to Lyndon B. Johnson, who supported the space program while in the Senate, Kennedy held off on his plans to dismantle the program.[cxxxiii]

President Kennedy's opinions on the space program changed on 12 April 1961 when Yuri Gagarin, a Soviet cosmonaut, became the first person to fly into space. This advancement increased American fears about being left behind the Soviet Union in regard to technological competition.[cxxxiv] Feeling the same sentiment as most of his people, President Kennedy grew eager for the United States to push by the Soviet Union to take the lead in what was dubbed the Space Race so that the country could maintain its strategy and prestige.

Kennedy sent a memo to Johnson on 20 April that asked him to look into the American space program and try to figure out how to help it catch up to the Soviet Union. Johnson checked with a few people whose judgment he trusted before replying a week later: "We are neither making maximum effort nor achieving results necessary if this country is to reach a position of leadership." Ted Sorensen told Kennedy that he should make great efforts in order to support the space program if it were to succeed in landing a person on the moon. On 25 May, Kennedy announced the lofty goal in his speech "Special Message to the Congress on Urgent National Needs":

"I believe that this nation should commit itself to achieving the goal, before this decade is out, of landing a man on the Moon and returning him safely to the Earth. No single space project in this period will be more impressive to mankind, or more important for the long-range exploration of space, and none will be so difficult or expensive to accomplish. We propose to accelerate the development of the appropriate lunar spacecraft. We propose to develop alternate liquid and solid fuel boosters, much larger than any now being developed, until certain which is superior. We propose additional funds for other engine development and for unmanned explorations—explorations which are particularly important for one purpose which this nation will never overlook: the survival of the man who first makes this daring flight. But in a very real sense, it will not be one man going to the moon—if we make this judgment affirmatively, it will be an entire nation. For all of us must work to put him there."

When Congress authorized the necessary funding, James E. Webb, the NASA administrator under President Kennedy, started the long process of reorganizing NASA though increasing the program's staffing level and building two new centers: a Launch Operations Center for the large moon rocket northwest of Cape Canaveral Air Force Station and a Manned Spacecraft Center on land that Rice University donated in Houston, Texas.

In light of Rice's donation, President Kennedy delivered a speech at their university on 12 September 1962 in an effort to promote the space program. He said:

"If this capsule history of our progress teaches us anything, it is that man, in his quest for knowledge and progress, is determined and cannot be deterred. The exploration of space will go ahead, whether we join in it or not, and it is one of the great adventures of all time, and no nation which expects to be the leader of other nations can expect to stay behind in this race for space.

Those who came before us made certain that this country rode the first waves of the industrial revolution, the first waves of modern invention, and the first wave of nuclear power and this generation does not intend to founder in the backwash of the coming age of space. We mean to be a part of it—we mean to lead it. For the eyes of the world now look into space, to the moon and to the planets beyond, and we have vowed that we shall not see it governed by a hostile flag of conquest, but by a banner of freedom and peace. We have vowed that we shall not see space filled with weapons of mass destruction, but with instruments of knowledge and understanding.

Yet the vows of this Nation can only be fulfilled if we in this Nation are first, and, therefore, we intend to be first. In short, our leadership in science and industry, our hopes for peace and security, our obligations to ourselves as well as others, all require us to make this effort, to solve these mysteries, to solve them for the good of all men, and to become the world's leading space-faring nation."

Kennedy was making an argument and formulating it well. He knew what he wanted for the United States and planned to deliver it. Almost six years after Kennedy's death, on 20 July 1969, Apollo 11 landed the first manned spacecraft on the Moon.

Chapter Nine: Assassination

Perhaps the most well-known fact about President John F. Kennedy is that he met an untimely end before his presidency was over. At 12:30 in the afternoon on Friday, 22 November 1963, President Kennedy was assassinated in Dallas, Texas, where he had traveled to attempt smoothing over frictions between two Democratic politicians in Texas. Kennedy was shot twice, once through the back and again in the head. America gasped loudly and wept for the young leader.

JFK was in a motorcade, sitting beside his wife in the back of an open car as they waved to the surrounding crowd. Soon after they turned a corner, two gunshots rang out over the crowd. People at the scene recall thinking that a motorcycle had backfired. When Jacqueline saw her husband slumped down beside her, she panicked, attempting to collect a piece of his skull that had become detached. Kennedy was rushed to Parkland Hospital for emergency medical treatment, but the surgeries were unsuccessful. The President of the United States died thirty minutes later. At the time of death, President Kennedy was 46 years old and had been serving as the president for a little over 1,000 days.

Lee Harvey Oswald was arrested for the murder, but denied shooting and claimed he was framed. Before he could be prosecuted for the shooting, he was killed by Jack Ruby on 24 November. Ruby was arrested and convicted of Oswald's murder, but he successfully appealed his conviction only to die of cancer on 3 January 1967, before he could attend his new trial.

Lyndon B. Johnson was quickly sworn into office while Jacqueline Kennedy stood next to him. Through an executive order, he created the Warren Commission, which was under the control of Chief Justice Earl Warren. The sole purpose of the Commission was to investigate the assassination. In conclusion, they determined that Oswald acted alone in the murder and was part of no external or internal conspiracy.

America was feeling the effect of the assassination, and political repercussions were apparent. Even as late as 2004, a news poll showed that 66% of responding Americans thought the assassination was part of a larger conspiracy, and 74% thought there had been a cover-up in the government. In 1979, the United States House Select Committee on Assassinations said it thought "that Kennedy was probably assassinated as a result of a conspiracy. The committee was unable to identify the other gunmen or the extent of the conspiracy." Historian Carl M. Brauer argued in 2002 that the public's "fascination with the assassination may indicate a psychological denial of John F. Kennedy's death, a mass wish to…undo it."[cxxxv]

The Cathedral of St. Matthew of the Apostle held a Requiem mass for Kennedy on 25 November 1963. Father John J. Cavanaugh officiated the ceremony. Later, both of JFK's brothers—Robert and Ted Kennedy—had funerals modeled after his own. After the funeral, the president was buried in a small plot within Arlington National Cemetery. Over the next three years, it is estimated that 16 million people visited his grave to pay their respects. According to testimonies, "Alan Seeger's 'I Have a Rendezvous with Death' was one of John F. Kennedy's favorite poems and he often asked his wife to recite it." Unfortunately, Kennedy's meeting with Death came a little too soon in life.

It was only a short while after John F. Kennedy's death that his presidency came to be known as the Camelot Era. Only a week later, Jacqueline Kennedy said in a *Life* magazine interview with Theodore H. White: "Don't let it be forgot, that there was a spot, for one brief shining moment that was known as Camelot. There'll be great presidents again, but there will never be another Camelot."

JFK's assassination not only had a dreadful effect on the nation in regard to the people's safety consciousness, but it also affected other parts of society in less obvious ways. Kennedy, of course, was the first president to heavily utilize television for political gain. His death greatly showcased that fact. Coverage of his death was mostly given through television. Newspaper clippings of headlines on the assassination were kept as souvenirs rather than sources of the latest information. At the time of his death, all three major United States television networks suspended their scheduled timeslots to cover the death. For 70 hours, nothing was on television except for news of the assassination, which made this coverage the longest uninterrupted news story on American television until 9/11.

Just as people do now with 9/11 memories, people alive during the John F. Kennedy assassination recall where they were when they heard the news that he had been shot in Dallas. The United Nations Ambassador Adlai Stevenson said, "All of us…will bear the grief of his death until the day of ours." Even people who were not alive during the assassination are heavily affected by Kennedy's death. Conspiracy theorists still gather to discuss how Kennedy may have been involved in something about which no one knew, something no one was supposed to know.

Chapter Ten: Legacy

Decades after his death, people recall John F. Kennedy as a kind president who tried his best to do what he could to improve the lives of the American people. His funeral was a momentous event, bringing in representatives from over 90 countries. Specific groups of people recalled his influence on them, as well. The United States Special Forces reverently regarded their relationship with Kennedy. Forrest Lindley who wrote for the United States military newspaper *Stars and Stripes* said, "It was President Kennedy who was responsible for the rebuilding of the Special Forces and giving us back our Green Beret." Kennedy was the first of six presidents to have served in the United States Navy, as well, and one of his most noticeable contributions to the administration was his support of the creation of the Navy SEALs in 1961.[cxxxvi]

President Kennedy pushed the country toward what is possibly the most important turn in American history: the institution of the Civil Rights Act of 1964, which eventually ended the reign of racist terror in the "Solid South." He provided economic aid to South Vietnam, delivered iconic speeches, and inspired Americans to be better. President Kennedy successfully pushed America forward in the Space Race, curtailing Soviet efforts to rise above. After JFK's death, he was given the *Pacem in Terris* (Peace on Earth) Award. Needless to say, Kennedy's legacy will live on long after today. Although he was only in office for a short period of time, he is often voted as one of America's best presidents, alongside Abraham Lincoln, George Washington, and Franklin D. Roosevelt.

Check out another book by Captivating History

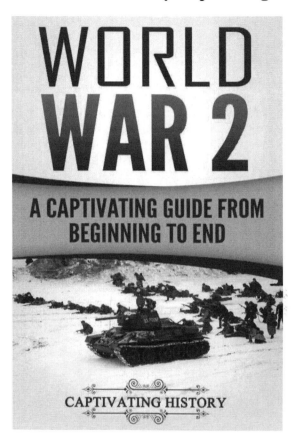

Make sure to check out more books by Captivating History

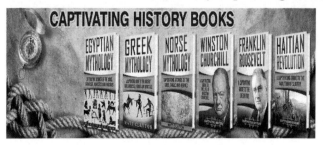

Free Bonus from Captivating History (Available for a Limited time)

Hi History Lovers!

Now you have a chance to join our exclusive history list so you can get your first history ebook for free as well as discounts and a potential to get more history books for free! Simply visit the link below to join.

Captivatinghistory.com/ebook

Also, make sure to follow us on:

Twitter: @Captivhistory

Facebook: Captivating History: @captivatinghistory

Primary and Secondary Sources

[i] *The Gallop Poll 1999*. Wilmington, Delaware: Scholarly Resources Inc. 1999. pp. 248–249.

[ii] Reeves, Richard. *President Kennedy: Profile of Power.* 1993.

[iii] Reeves, Richard. *President Kennedy: Profile of Power.* 1993.

[iv] "John F. Kennedy and Ireland." *John F. Kennedy Presidential Library and Museum.* https://www.jfklibrary.org/JFK/JFK-in-History/John-F-Kennedy-and-Ireland.aspx. Accessed 18 August 2017.

[v] O'Brien, Michael. *John F. Kennedy: A Biography.* 2005.

[vi] Failla, Zak. "Looking Back on JFK's Time in Bronxville." *The Daily Voice.* 18 November 2013.

[vii] Dallek, Robert. *An Unfinished Life: John F. Kennedy, 1917—1963.* 2003.

[viii] Kenney, Charles. *John F. Kennedy: The Presidential Portfolio.* 2000.

[ix] Dallek, Robert. "The Medical Ordeals of JFK." *The Atlantic.* December 2002. https://web.archive.org/web/20160811195843/http://www.theatlantic.com/magazine/archive/2002/12/the-medical-ordeals-of-jfk/305572/?single_page=true. 24 August 2017.

[x] Kenney, Charles. *John F. Kennedy: The Presidential Portfolio.* 2000.

[xi] Dallek, Robert. *An Unfinished Life: John F. Kennedy, 1917—1963.* 2003.

[xii] Barkhorn, Eleanor. "JFK's Very Revealing Harvard Application Essay." *The Atlantic.* 21 November 2013. https://www.theatlantic.com/education/archive/2013/11/jfks-very-revealing-harvard-application-essay/281699/. 25 August 2017.

[xiii] Clarke, John. "Selling J.F.K.'s Boat." *The New Yorker.* 19 May 2015.

[xiv] Dallek, Robert. *An Unfinished Life: John F. Kennedy, 1917—1963.* 2003.

[xv] Dallek, Robert. *An Unfinished Life: John F. Kennedy, 1917—1963.* 2003.

[xvi] Dallek, Robert. *An Unfinished Life: John F. Kennedy, 1917—1963.* 2003.

[xvii] Brinkley, Alan. *John F. Kennedy.* 2012.

[xviii] Kenney, Charles. *John F. Kennedy: The Presidential Portfolio.* 2000.

[xix] Kenney, Charles. *John F. Kennedy: The Presidential Portfolio*. 2000.

[xx] Dallek, Robert. *An Unfinished Life: John F. Kennedy, 1917—1963*. 2003.

[xxi] Dallek, Robert. "The Medical Ordeals of JFK." *The Atlantic*. December 2002. https://web.archive.org/web/20160811195843/http://www.theatlantic.com/magazine/archive/2002/12/the-medical-ordeals-of-jfk/305572/?single_page=true. 24 August 2017.

[xxii] Mandel, Lee R. "Endocrine and Autoimmune Aspects of the Health History of John F. Kennedy." *Annals of Internal Medicine*. 1 September 2009. http://annals.org/aim/article/744707/endocrine-autoimmune-aspects-health-history-john-f-kennedy#xref-ref-9-1. 1 September 2017.

[xxiii] Mandel, Lee R. "Endocrine and Autoimmune Aspects of the Health History of John F. Kennedy." *Annals of Internal Medicine*. 1 September 2009. http://annals.org/aim/article/744707/endocrine-autoimmune-aspects-health-history-john-f-kennedy#xref-ref-9-1. 1 September 2017.

[xxiv] Kempe, Frederick. *Berlin 1961*. 2012.

[xxv] Reeves, Richard. *President Kennedy: Profile of Power*. 1993.

[xxvi] Reeves, Richard. *President Kennedy: Profile of Power*. 1993.

[xxvii] Dallek, Robert. *An Unfinished Life: John F. Kennedy, 1917—1963*. 2003.

[xxviii] Osborne, Robert. *Leading Ladies: The 50 Most Unforgettable Actresses of the Studio Era*. 2006.

[xxix] Dallek, Robert. *An Unfinished Life: John F. Kennedy, 1917—1963*. 2003.

[xxx] Reeves, Richard. *President Kennedy: Profile of Power*. 1993.

[xxxi] Reeves, Richard. *President Kennedy: Profile of Power*. 1993.

[xxxii] Donovan, Robert J. *PT-109: John F. Kennedy in WW II*. 2001.

[xxxiii] Donovan, Robert J. *PT-109: John F. Kennedy in WW II*. 2001.

[xxxiv] O'Brien, Michael. *John F. Kennedy: A Biography*. 2005.

[xxxv] Dallek, Robert. *An Unfinished Life: John F. Kennedy, 1917—1963*. 2003.

[xxxvi] Dallek, Robert. *An Unfinished Life: John F. Kennedy, 1917—1963*. 2003.

[xxxvii] Brinkley, Alan. *John F. Kennedy*. 2012.

[xxxviii] Brinkley, Alan. *John F. Kennedy*. 2012.

[xxxix] O'Brien, Michael. *John F. Kennedy: A Biography*. 2005.

xl O'Brien, Michael. *John F. Kennedy: A Biography*. 2005.

xli Brinkley, Alan. *John F. Kennedy*. 2012.

xlii Brinkley, Alan. *John F. Kennedy*. 2012.

xliii Brinkley, Alan. *John F. Kennedy*. 2012.

xliv Brinkley, Alan. *John F. Kennedy*. 2012.

xlv Reeves, Richard. *President Kennedy: Profile of Power*. 1993.

xlvi Reeves, Richard. *President Kennedy: Profile of Power*. 1993.

xlvii Kempe, Frederick. *Berlin 1961*. 2011.

xlviii Reeves, Richard. *President Kennedy: Profile of Power*. 1993.

xlix Reeves, Richard. *President Kennedy: Profile of Power*. 1993.

l Reeves, Richard. *President Kennedy: Profile of Power*. 1993.

li Reeves, Richard. *President Kennedy: Profile of Power*. 1993.

lii Reeves, Richard. *President Kennedy: Profile of Power*. 1993.

liii Schlesinger, Jr., Arthur M. *A Thousand Days: John F. Kennedy in the White House*. 2002.

liv Reeves, Richard. *President Kennedy: Profile of Power*. 1993.

lv Schlesinger, Jr., Arthur M. *A Thousand Days: John F. Kennedy in the White House*. 2002.

lvi Reeves, Richard. *President Kennedy: Profile of Power*. 1993.

lvii Reeves, Richard. *President Kennedy: Profile of Power*. 1993.

lviii Reeves, Richard. *President Kennedy: Profile of Power*. 1993.

lix Reeves, Richard. *President Kennedy: Profile of Power*. 1993.

lx Reeves, Richard. *President Kennedy: Profile of Power*. 1993.

lxi Reeves, Richard. *President Kennedy: Profile of Power*. 1993.

lxii Reeves, Richard. *President Kennedy: Profile of Power*. 1993.

lxiii Kenney, Charles. *John F. Kennedy: The Presidential Portfolio*. 2000.

lxiv Reeves, Richard. *President Kennedy: Profile of Power*. 1993.

lxv Schlesinger, Jr., Arthur M. *A Thousand Days: John F. Kennedy in the White House*. 2002.

[lxvi] Reeves, Richard. *President Kennedy: Profile of Power.* 1993.

[lxvii] Reeves, Richard. *President Kennedy: Profile of Power.* 1993.

[lxviii] Dallek, Robert. *An Unfinished Life: John F. Kennedy, 1917—1963.* 2003.

[lxix] Schlesinger, Jr., Arthur M. *A Thousand Days: John F. Kennedy in the White House.* 2002.

[lxx] Meisler, Stanley. *When the World Calls: The Inside Story of the Peace Corps and Its First Fifty Years.* 2011.

[lxxi] Reeves, Richard. *President Kennedy: Profile of Power.* 1993.

[lxxii] Reeves, Richard. *President Kennedy: Profile of Power.* 1993.

[lxxiii] Dunnigan, James, and Albert Nofi. *Dirty Little Secrets of the Vietnam War.* 1999.

[lxxiv] Reeves, Richard. *President Kennedy: Profile of Power.* 1993.

[lxxv] Reeves, Richard. *President Kennedy: Profile of Power.* 1993.

[lxxvi] Reeves, Richard. *President Kennedy: Profile of Power.* 1993.

[lxxvii] Reeves, Richard. *President Kennedy: Profile of Power.* 1993.

[lxxviii] Reeves, Richard. *President Kennedy: Profile of Power.* 1993.

[lxxix] Reeves, Richard. *President Kennedy: Profile of Power.* 1993.

[lxxx] Reeves, Richard. *President Kennedy: Profile of Power.* 1993.

[lxxxi] Reeves, Richard. *President Kennedy: Profile of Power.* 1993.

[lxxxii] Reeves, Richard. *President Kennedy: Profile of Power.* 1993.

[lxxxiii] Reeves, Richard. *President Kennedy: Profile of Power.* 1993.

[lxxxiv] Reeves, Richard. *President Kennedy: Profile of Power.* 1993.

[lxxxv] Talbot, David. "Warrior for Peace." *Time Magazine.* 21 June 2007.

[lxxxvi] Matthews, Chris. *Jack Kennedy: Elusive Hero.* 2011.

[lxxxvii] Sorensen, Theodore. *Kennedy.* 1965.

[lxxxviii] Reeves, Richard. *President Kennedy: Profile of Power.* 1993.

[lxxxix] Reeves, Richard. *President Kennedy: Profile of Power.* 1993

[xc] Dallek, Robert. *An Unfinished Life: John F. Kennedy, 1917—1963.* 2003.

[xci] Reeves, Richard. *President Kennedy: Profile of Power.* 1993

[xcii] Walt, Stephen M. *The Origins of Alliances*. 1987.

[xciii] Salt, Jeremey. *The Unmaking of the Middle East: A History of Western Disorder in Arab Lands*. 2008.

[xciv] Salt, Jeremey. *The Unmaking of the Middle East: A History of Western Disorder in Arab Lands*. 2008.

[xcv] Hersh, Seymour. *The Dark Side of Camelot*. 1997.

[xcvi] Salt, Jeremey. *The Unmaking of the Middle East: A History of Western Disorder in Arab Lands*. 2008.

[xcvii] Salt, Jeremey. *The Unmaking of the Middle East: A History of Western Disorder in Arab Lands*. 2008.

[xcviii] Hersh, Seymour. *The Dark Side of Camelot*. 1997.

[xcix] Trachtenberg, Marc. *A Constructed Peace: The Making of the European Settlement, 1945—1963*. 8 February 1999.

[c] Gibson, Bryan R. *Sold Out? US Foreign Policy, Iraq, the Kurds, and the Cold War*. 2015.

[ci] Gibson, Bryan R. *Sold Out? US Foreign Policy, Iraq, the Kurds, and the Cold War*. 2015.

[cii] Gibson, Bryan R. *Sold Out? US Foreign Policy, Iraq, the Kurds, and the Cold War*. 2015.

[ciii] Reeves, Richard. *President Kennedy: Profile of Power*. 1993

[civ] Frum, David. *How We Got Here: The '70s*. 2000.

[cv] Frum, David. *How We Got Here: The '70s*. 2000.

[cvi] Reeves, Richard. *President Kennedy: Profile of Power*. 1993.

[cvii] O'Brien, Michael. *John F. Kennedy: A Biography*. 2005.

[cviii] Reeves, Richard. *President Kennedy: Profile of Power*. 1993.

[cix] Reeves, Richard. *President Kennedy: Profile of Power*. 1993.

[cx] Grantham. *The Life and Death of the Solid South: A Political History*. 1988.

[cxi] Dallek, Robert. *An Unfinished Life: John F. Kennedy, 1917—1963*. 2003.

[cxii] Dallek, Robert. *An Unfinished Life: John F. Kennedy, 1917—1963*. 2003.

[cxiii] Brauer, Carl M. "John F. Kennedy." *The Presidents: A Reference History*. edited by Henry Graff. 2002.

[cxiv] Brauer, Carl M. "John F. Kennedy." *The Presidents: A Reference History.* edited by Henry Graff. 2002.

[cxv] Bryant, Nick. "Black Man Who Was Crazy Enough to Apply to Ole Miss." *The Journal of Blacks in Higher Education.* Autumn 2006.

[cxvi] Brauer, Carl M. "John F. Kennedy." *The Presidents: A Reference History.* edited by Henry Graff. 2002.

[cxvii] Reeves, Richard. *President Kennedy: Profile of Power.* 1993.

[cxviii] Brauer, Carl M. "John F. Kennedy." *The Presidents: A Reference History.* edited by Henry Graff. 2002.

[cxix] Bryant, Nick. "Black Man Who Was Crazy Enough to Apply to Ole Miss." *The Journal of Blacks in Higher Education.* Autumn 2006.

[cxx] Dallek, Robert. *An Unfinished Life: John F. Kennedy, 1917—1963.* 2003.

[cxxi] Reeves, Richard. *President Kennedy: Profile of Power.* 1993.

[cxxii] Reeves, Richard. *President Kennedy: Profile of Power.* 1993.

[cxxiii] Reeves, Richard. *President Kennedy: Profile of Power.* 1993.

[cxxiv] Schlesinger, Jr., Arthur M. *A Thousand Days: John F. Kennedy in the White House.* 2002.

[cxxv] Cohen, Andrew. *Two Days in June: John F. Kennedy and the 48 Hours That Changed History.* 2014.

[cxxvi] Goduti, Jr., Philip A. *Robert F. Kennedy and the Shaping of Civil Rights, 1960-1964.* 2012.

[cxxvii] Reeves, Richard. *President Kennedy: Profile of Power.* 1993.

[cxxviii] Reeves, Richard. *President Kennedy: Profile of Power.* 1993.

[cxxix] Reeves, Richard. *President Kennedy: Profile of Power.* 1993.

[cxxx] Brauer, Carl M. "John F. Kennedy." *The Presidents: A Reference History.* edited by Henry Graff. 2002.

[cxxxi] Reeves, Richard. *President Kennedy: Profile of Power.* 1993.

[cxxxii] Dallek, Robert. *An Unfinished Life: John F. Kennedy, 1917—1963.* 2003.

[cxxxiii] Reeves, Richard. *President Kennedy: Profile of Power.* 1993.

[cxxxiv] Dallek, Robert. *An Unfinished Life: John F. Kennedy, 1917—1963.* 2003.

[cxxxv] Brauer, Carl M. "John F. Kennedy." *The Presidents: A Reference History.* edited by Henry Graff. 2002.

[cxxxvi] Salinger, Pierre. *John F. Kennedy: Commander in Chief: A Profile in Leadership.* 1997.

Franklin Roosevelt: